From Misfit
To Purpose

From Misfit To Purpose

ISBN: 979-8-9883724-7-9 (paperback)
         979-8-9883724-8-6 (ebook)

Printed in the United States of America

From Misfit
To Purpose

ALEXANDRIA PAGE

1

Life's beauty lies in the tapestry woven from moments, memories, and stories. Amidst the rush, we sometimes fixate on the negatives, overlooking the splendor within each narrative. Life's journey is an ever-shifting adventure; it transforms in a breath, captivates in an instant. Acknowledging the occasional hardships and heartaches doesn't negate the intrinsic goodness. Amidst trials, there's the charm of love, the allure of adventure, or the solace of a serene stroll on the beach—experiences that nourish the soul. I'm realizing that the richness of existence is found in these simple moments we often overlook. Amidst the hustle, pausing to breathe and just be can uncover profound beauty.

2

Losing my father was one of the most challenging things I've ever faced. Now, as I navigate the darkness once more, I find purpose. I discovered an unforeseen gift—writing. Poetry and inspiring words flowed from me, a talent I never knew I possessed. In the aftermath, I grappled with finding a new normal, a place of belonging. Those experiences molded me into who I am today. The lonely moments offered wisdom about my father, about myself, far beyond any book. He foresaw my gift and kindled it. My first journal, a gift from my grandmother, became the blueprint of my destiny. My first poem, recited nervously in church, unveiled my calling. It was in my vulnerability that God displayed his beauty. Embracing uncertainty and taking leaps of faith has led to unexpected blessings. God's plans are unstoppable, even in the face of setbacks and deceit. He remains faithful.

3

At just 7 years old, darkness threatened to steal my innocence. A friend's brother invaded my boundaries, but my cousin, a guardian angel, intervened. Her protective stance saved me, a divine presence in a bleak moment. The memory lingers, but I refuse to let it define me. For those enduring similar pain, know this moment doesn't determine your worth. It's vital not to let it fester, to confide in your support system, and to seek healing—be it through counseling, therapy, or the unwavering love of family. Remember, this experience is part of your story, not your identity. Don't bear the weight alone; release it, and find your freedom.

4

Amidst the agony of my father's passing, I sought meaning in the pain. Yet again, life had thrown me into a realm of loss. Denying the inevitable, I held onto hope for his healing. However, I came to understand that certain pain can't be outrun; it just is. Through these agonizing journeys, I learned my most beautiful life lessons. Romans 8:28 became a comforting truth: all things work together for good. My dad's passing reaffirmed that life is fleeting, but also precious. Amidst despair, there's grace, waiting to guide us through storms. While I didn't comprehend God's ways, I trusted His love would sustain me. His grace carried me through the darkest moments, teaching me that healing isn't instant; it's a gradual emergence into the light.

5

My life, though imperfect, is blessed. People often question how I find the strength to smile despite my tribulations. The answer lies in my unwavering faith—a foundation laid upon God's love. No matter the earthly relationships I've lost, God remains my constant father. His hand supports me, catches me when I fall. Even in my weakest moments, His grace uplifts me. Though I grieve my losses, I'm guided by faith, hope, and love—a big extended family that transcends blood relations. It's this family, this faith, that helps me find purpose and positivity amidst life's trials.

6

If I could address my younger self, I'd say: Embrace authenticity, cease striving to fit in, for you were designed to stand out. Cherish the present, don't dwell on an uncertain future. Life's hardships are lessons shaping your character. Forgiving, even in the face of unspeakable pain, brings freedom. God's grace empowers you to extend mercy, just as you've received it. Looking back is a measure of growth, not regret. Every scar, every misstep, contributes to your unique journey. Embrace who you are, for you're a masterpiece in God's hands.

7

Amidst the struggle, I found compassion where anger once thrived. Face to face with the man who took my mother, I felt God's grace flowing within me. His presence extinguished my anger, replacing it with an unexpected empathy. This transformation wasn't my doing—it was God's work. I forgave him, not for his sake, but to free myself. My faith taught me that extending grace mirrors the love God showers upon us. Through this experience, I recognized the imprints of Christ in my life.

8

Though loss has shaped my journey, I'm thankful for the love and lessons woven into my life's fabric. From church family to blood relatives, their support has been unwavering. They've embraced me during life's storms, ensuring I don't bear my burdens alone. My upbringing gifted me with compassion and kindness, as my experiences refined my character. These relationships, both cherished and endured, form the foundation upon which I've built my life.

9

Looking back is about seeing progress, not harboring regrets. Each scar, mistake, and challenge has contributed to my growth. The past isn't an anchor but a guide, steering me away from pitfalls. It's a rearview mirror, offering perspective as I move forward. I've learned to treasure what God has done, even amidst difficulties. I embrace the fullness of life, aware that every chapter contributes to the masterpiece He's crafting.

10

The past is a mirror reflecting growth, not a prison of regrets. God's grace has brought me far, and it's only by acknowledging this journey that I appreciate His transformative power. Each scar, every twist and turn, contributes to my story's richness. Regret is a futile emotion when God's guidance has steered me through life's maze. Embrace the past for its lessons, and look to the future with hope, knowing He's walking beside you.

11

Many people ask how I found the strength to confront the man who took my mother's life. However, my connection with him dates back to my childhood; he was once my mother's boyfriend. Undertaking such a task seemed nearly impossible, yet when God's call transcends your natural mindset, it challenges your very core. Recognizing this was divine guidance, I braced myself for a mission that defied my comfort zone. How could I sit across from a man who had shattered my foundation, my identity, and the irreplaceable love only a mother can provide? Despite the presence of supportive family members, their love couldn't fill the void left by a mother's absence.

But with God's grace, I summoned supernatural strength to tackle the seemingly insurmountable. I was reluctant, plagued by internal turmoil, reminiscent of Jacob wrestling with an angel. Ultimately, I surrendered to God's plan, realizing this journey was etched in my destiny. In a defining moment, I gazed upwards, silently conveying my willingness. The still, small voice within assured me, reassuring me I was merely a vessel for His purpose.

Taking those daunting steps, I approached the man who had taken so much from me. The gravity of that encounter transcended words, as God's unseen hands steadied me. The power to sit across

From Misfit To Purpose

from him, to engage in conversation, originated not from my own strength, but from divine intervention. The decision was agonizing, yet my faith buoyed me. This encounter wasn't about erasing the pain; it was about extending the grace and love that only God's empowerment could provide.

12

Navigating a new normal at seven years old, after the abrupt loss of my mother, was a challenge no child should face. That day, as I boarded the school bus with an unsuspecting farewell, little did I know it was our final exchange. The absence of a mother's nurturing presence shook the foundations of my identity. A mother's embrace, her guidance, was irreplaceable, forever shaping my path.

Family, friends, and community played vital roles, bridging the void to some extent. Their support cushioned my journey through an unfamiliar life. Yet, the ache persisted—living in a movie that wasn't mine, learning to navigate uncharted waters. Emergence from innocence into the reality of life's fragility was jarring. Fire trucks, police, media converged around my home, illuminating the truth that life had irrevocably changed.

I vividly recall firefighters striving to distract me from the scene, offering momentary respite. They sensed the impending collapse of my world. That day, innocence was replaced by harsh reality. Struggling to comprehend, I observed my father's anguish, sensing that something grievous had occurred. The revelation came later, delivered through tear-filled eyes—my mother was gone, taken by God's embrace. Processing such a loss at seven defies comprehension. Numbness shielded me from its full weight, yet it would ultimately yield to a path of healing and acceptance, albeit through the crucible of pain.

13

From childhood, I gazed at other children with their mothers, aching for the same bond. Amid blessings of family and community, the absence of a mother's embrace created an enduring ache. I often withdrew, feeling misplaced, the odd one out. As I matured, I realized my uniqueness was my strength, a divine creation not tethered to societal molds.

14

Numbness seemed a refuge, a means to escape the overwhelming pain. Yet, the journey taught me that true strength doesn't stem from avoidance but from facing pain head-on. Strength is found in allowing yourself to hurt, to endure, and to heal. The path was littered with questions, moments of despair, yet through the brokenness, growth emerged.

15

Childhood should be sheltered from goodbyes, but I was thrust into the art of farewells at an early age. The memory of visiting my mother's grave while barely comprehending the gravity remains etched. The weight of that moment lingered, shaping my future.

16

On September 15, 1992, my world shifted irrevocably. A mere seven-year-old, I bade my mother farewell, blissfully unaware it would be forever. Transitioning from anticipated family moments to the somber reality of absence marked the beginning of a new chapter.

17

Forgiveness isn't a sign of weakness; it's a testament to strength. Through forgiveness, we unshackle ourselves from the past's hold. The choice to forgive is a testament to the courage of our hearts. While difficult, it liberates us from the prison of resentment, granting us the freedom to embrace love and the present.

18

The journey of forgiveness defied my expectations. Sitting across from the man who forever altered my life was a surreal experience. Yet, he wasn't the monster I envisioned. In his brokenness, I glimpsed God's transformative power. Forgiving him wasn't just for him; it liberated me from the chains of hatred.

19

The notion of forgiving the unforgivable seemed unthinkable. Yet, divine strength emerged, unearthing a wellspring of courage. I embarked on a journey to face the past, determined to release the hold it had on me. Forgiveness was a personal decision that liberated me from my own captivity.

20

The act of forgiving seemed incomprehensible, a monumental task that lay beyond human capacity. Yet, divine intervention breathed life into my resolve. Relinquishing my hatred set me free from a cycle of pain, allowing me to reclaim my life's narrative. By embracing forgiveness, I unearthed strength that transcended the limits of my humanity.

Printed in the USA
CPSIA information can be obtained
at www.ICGtesting.com
LVHW050338090224
771178LV00001B/187